This book belongs to

....

It was given to me by

....

On this date

....

JONAH & ME

Devotions for Boys

Glenn Hascall

BARBOUR kidz
A Division of Barbour Publishing

ISBN 979-8-89151-122-4

Cover illustrations by Pedro Riquelme

Published by Barbour Publishing, Inc., 1810 Barbour Drive, Uhrichsville, Ohio 44683, www.barbourbooks.com

Our mission is to inspire the world with the life-changing message of the Bible.

Printed in China.

002479 0525 DS

Welcome to

JONAH & ME

Devotions for Boys!

The story of Jonah is just four chapters long—and they're not long chapters. Jonah's big story seems simple enough: He was given a job. He chose not to do it. God corrected him. Then Jonah obeyed, but with a bad attitude.

There's much more to learn from his story. You may even discover that there have been times when you've been a little (or a lot) like Jonah.

He found it hard to obey God, hard to be grateful, and hard to watch the Lord show kindness to others. Jonah knew a lot, but he still had more to learn. It may not look as if Jonah offers a very good example, but when you read his story carefully, you'll find a lot of things you should do and not do.

Take your time and think about what you learn.

A page-turning adventure is waiting, but there's a lot to think about.

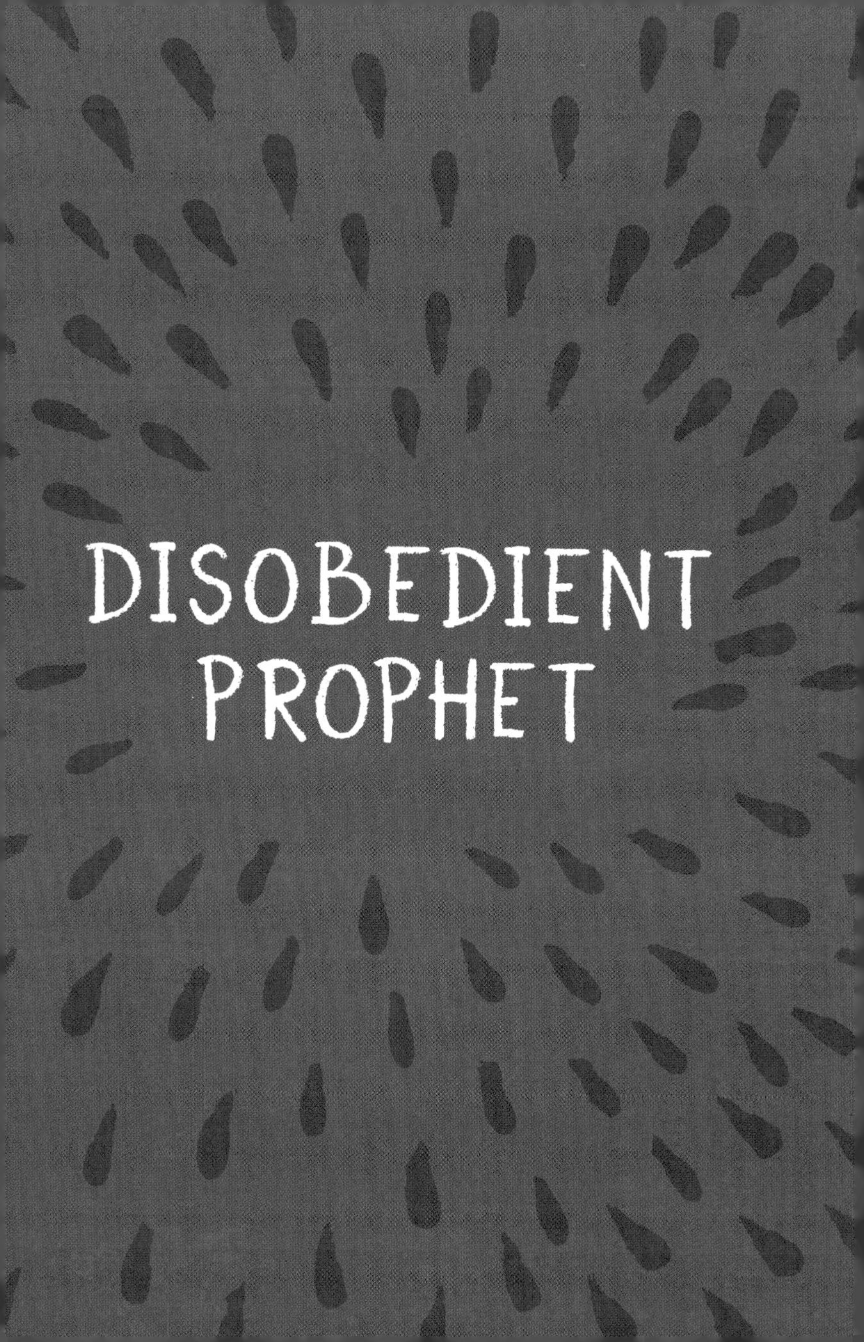
DISOBEDIENT
PROPHET

JUST ONE JOB

[God said to Jonah,] "Get up and go to the large city of Nineveh, and preach against it. For their sin has come up before Me."

JONAH 1:2 NLV

Jonah had a job. He was a prophet, someone who shared God's messages with people. Once upon a time, he must have been good at his job. When God gave Jonah messages, he usually delivered them. People needed to hear them.

When your mom asks you to tell a brother or sister that it's time to eat, you share what you've been told. And it's a good thing for everybody. Your brother or sister are happy because they know when to eat. Your mom is happy because you obeyed. You are happy because you could be trusted to do what your mom asked.

You might be a messenger for your mom, and that's your job. If you decide not to share that message, you're not doing your job very well. It won't make your mom happy. It doesn't make God happy. That's the way it was for Jonah. He didn't obey God, and that was sin.

If you choose to disobey, you might just learn that Jonah was very much like you. He had a choice to make, but would he make the right one?

There are a lot of choices
I can make, Lord. I want to
make the choices that You
would make. Help me to obey.
Help me to remember that's
what You want. When I forget,
help me to admit I was wrong.

CHOICES

But Jonah rose up to flee to Tarshish from the presence of the Lord *and went down to Joppa.*

Jonah 1:3 SKJV

After you make a wrong choice, you might learn to make a better choice. You might learn to admit you were wrong. You can decide to turn around and walk with God.

It was hard for Jonah to admit he was wrong. So he continued to make bad choices.

First, he ran from God. Jonah knew what direction he wanted to go. It was far away from where God wanted him to go. God had said that he should go east to Nineveh. But Jonah bought a ticket to Tarshish, in the west. God gave Jonah a message, but Jonah wanted to keep it a secret. What was that message? God wanted the people of Nineveh to stop sinning and make better choices. He wanted them to know that He was God.

Jonah knew God wanted people to obey Him. Yet this prophet made the choice to do something other than what God told him to do. Does it seem strange? Why would Jonah do that? Why might you?

It's easy to think that my choices don't mean anything, God. But the story of Jonah shows me that when You tell me what to do, I can obey or I can make a wrong choice. Help me to do what You want me to do, Lord. Help me to obey.

PAYING TO AVOID GOD

Jonah paid money. . .
to get away from the Lord.

Jonah 1:3 NLV

It's an honor when God asks you to do something. The God who made you has a plan for your life. He gives you the opportunity to agree with His plan.

For example, God asks you to honor your parents, which means that you respect them in what you choose to say and what you decide to do. You pay attention to the things you learn from them. You allow the good things they teach to help you make good choices.

Jonah had the chance to respect God in what he said and did. But instead of making a good choice, he paid money to get away from the Lord.

This man who worked for God wanted to get away from God so badly that he paid to try.

God has given you everything. He gave you air to breathe, food to eat, and water to drink. More than anything else, God offers you His love. Why run from Him? Why pay to avoid Him? Why would you want to?

Jonah had his reasons, but they were horrible ones. Keep reading, because this is a story that takes bad decisions and explains God's forgiveness. He loves to give second chances.

I will never be able to pay for all the good things You've given me, Father. Don't let me spend my money running away from You. When I remember that You gave me everything, help me to give You my respect and obedience.

BRAGGING ABOUT DISOBEDIENCE

The men knew that [Jonah] fled from the presence of the Lord because he had told them.

Jonah 1:10 skjv

The ship was ready to leave Joppa for Tarshish. Jonah was on that ship. He was running away from God. He decided to tell the ship's crew that he was running from God. He may have made it seem as if it were a good idea to disobey God. But he was making another wrong choice.

Maybe you've heard other people bragging about their disobedience. They had something good to do, but they said no. They thought their disobedience was a good story to tell other people.

What if people hear you talking about disobeying God, and then they choose to disobey God? Have you helped them? Everyone needs a good example, but this was a lesson Jonah still needed to learn. You might know this is true, but a reminder is a very good idea.

A word that fits what Jonah was doing is *rebellion.* This word means you don't think God should be in charge. The things you do are telling God that you won't follow Him. Rebellion is a choice that makes God sad.

Telling anyone that making a bad choice is a good idea is rebellion, Lord. Jonah made this choice, and it must have made You very sad. Bragging about breaking Your rules is another bad idea. I want to come back to You whenever I make a bad choice.

FISH FOOD!

WELCOME TO TIME-OUT

*The Lord sent a big fish
to swallow Jonah.*

Jonah 1:17 NLV

If you've ever had an aquarium, you know that if you sprinkle food on top of the water, the fish will quickly swim upward, looking for a meal.

Jonah may have seemed like yummy fish food. A storm was making the sea splash with giant waves. Rain fell from dark clouds. Jonah told the ship's crew that he was the reason God sent the storm. He said they should toss him into the water.

The sailors now knew that Jonah had made a very bad choice. Jonah made a big splash as they tossed him into the sea.

This man who was given a message knew he was wrong for running away.

He knew God was not happy. He probably didn't know that God was sending a big fish to give him a time-out. One moment Jonah was tossed on the waves of a storm and the next he was listening to a fish's stomach making noises in the dark. It was time to think about how he had not obeyed God and the better choices he should have made.

You give me time to think, God. Help me to think good thoughts and make good choices. I want to learn to obey and to admit it when I don't. Thanks for loving me enough to keep encouraging me.

FISH STEW

Jonah was in the belly of the fish three days and three nights.

Jonah 1:17 SKJV

Big sea fish eat things like smaller fish and shrimp. This means that the stomach of the big fish where Jonah found himself was like a gurgling pot of fish stew. It probably didn't smell very good. Maybe Jonah was happy that it was dark, so he didn't have to see it.

There was nothing else for Jonah to do, so one of the first things he did was pray. He finally talked to the God he'd been running from. He recognized that trying to avoid God is never a good idea.

It can be easy to be distracted and not think about what God wants. You might choose to do anything else first. You should be considering good choices. But you're thinking about bad choices you'd rather make.

If God gives you a time-out, He's giving you a chance to focus on Him. You probably won't land in a fish belly. But suddenly you will have lots of time to think about choices. That's one of the reasons time-outs can be helpful.

Everyone has had time-outs. If you're anything like Jonah, you need one sometimes.

I don't like time-outs, Father. They seem like something that wastes my time and makes me unhappy. Thanks for reminding me that Jonah had a time-out. It made him interested in thinking about the choices he'd made. Please help me with the choices I need to make.

SEEKING GOD IN THE DARK

[Jonah prayed,] "I have been sent away from Your eyes. But I will look again toward Your holy house."

JONAH 2:4 NLV

Do you know anyone who was swallowed by a fish? No? Jonah probably didn't know anyone like that either. He probably wondered if he would ever see sunshine again. Would he ever carry a message from God again? Had his bad choice been his last choice?

Maybe you've made mistakes that seemed so bad that you wondered if it meant no one could ever love you again. If so, the story of Jonah is a really good story to think about.

Jonah wondered if God would ever pay attention to him again. Jonah didn't really understand God's love. But Jonah knew that God was more important than the message he had refused to take to Nineveh. God is big, and He could still get His message to those people.

In the fish's stomach, Jonah probably didn't believe that he would still be the one to take this message, sharing it with people he didn't even like.

It's hard to think I can be useful after I admit I've been wrong, Lord. I might believe that You'll never use me, when I've disobeyed. But You keep encouraging me to come closer to You. Then I can learn what to do, when to do it, and how.

SUDDENLY WILLING TO DELIVER

The L*ORD* *spoke to the fish, and it vomited out Jonah on the dry land.*

JONAH 2:10 SKJV

Everyone looks forward to the moment when a time-out is over. Like most people, once a time-out ends, you may believe you learned your lesson. You feel as if every new choice you make is going to be really good. Maybe that's how Jonah felt when God sent that big fish to the seashore and had it spit Jonah out onto the beach.

Jonah probably looked a little strange after a three-day bath in fish stew. But he had a message to share. Suddenly he was willing to deliver that message. The people of Nineveh needed to turn to God. But Jonah needed to follow God first. He knew the people had to make a choice. Would they make the right one? He had seen what happened when he made a bad choice.

Even though Jonah got a second chance, he still didn't really want the people of Nineveh to have a second chance. They were enemies of his country.

There was one word God had told Jonah to say. Now the messenger was ready to say it. "Repent." This meant to stop sinning. God wanted them to admit they sinned and turn to follow Him.

I'm grateful for second chances, God. The next time I have a choice, I have the chance to do the right thing. Thanks for helping me, because I will always need Your help.

FINALLY
FAITHFUL

THEY WERE READY TO HEAR

Jonah got up and went to Nineveh,
as the Lord had told him.

JONAH 3:3 NLV

It took three days to walk through the big city of Nineveh. More than one hundred thousand people lived there. Jonah would have to share God's message many times.

Maybe Jonah was surprised, but the people listened to him. They took him seriously. They learned that God loved them and wanted them to live for Him. God asked them to make better choices. They thought it was a good idea to listen and make changes in their lives.

The people took their own time-out. They stopped eating because they needed time to think about what it meant to quit doing what they were doing. As Jonah walked through Nineveh, the people were ready to hear what he would say. Then they started doing something new and something better. They did what God asked them to do.

How does it feel when you know you're doing the right thing? How can it make you feel closer to God? How will it help you make the next really good choice?

God does not always ask you to do something that's easy. But He always helps you do even the hardest things. Jonah learned that. You can learn from Jonah.

I want to be ready to listen to You, Father. Help me get ready to listen to what You say and do what You ask. Your messages are best, and following them will always be my next great idea.

A CHANGING OF CHOICES

[Nineveh's king said,] "Everyone must pray to God with all his heart, so each person may turn from his sinful way and from the bad things he has done."

JONAH 3:8 NLV

Jonah was finally doing what God asked him to do. This means the prophet was faithful to God for the first time in this story. And because Jonah did what God wanted, the people of Nineveh listened. They wanted to do what God wanted them to do, too. The king of Nineveh knew his kingdom was in trouble unless the people listened to God's message.

Jonah was telling everyone to turn around and walk in God's direction. So was the king. The king asked people to pray and really mean it. The king wanted people to notice the wrong things they had done. He wanted them to turn away from all the things they thought made those choices a good idea.

It had never been a good choice to fight against God. Jonah probably thought he understood that. The people of Nineveh were learning that. Things were changing in Nineveh. Jonah finally spoke the truth, and the people listened.

You have so many good things that You want people to know, Lord. I want to be faithful enough to learn what You want, do what You ask, and share what I learn. Help me to be a faithful messenger by learning Your message.

[The king of Nineveh said,]
"Who can tell if God will turn. . .
. . away from His fierce anger?"

JONAH 3:9 SKJV

Jonah gave a message that God wanted the people of Nineveh to hear. Those who heard the message took it seriously. Jonah was closer to God than the people of Nineveh were, but the people who heard the message were more concerned about doing the right thing than Jonah had been.

Maybe the king had heard stories of God's mercy. Mercy is when God stops a bad thing from happening to people who deserve punishment. What if God would be kind enough to forgive the people and give them time to make better choices?

How could it change things for people

today if they knew God gives second chances? He does. Could you tell them?

Jonah changed his mind and gave the people the message they needed to hear. But keep reading. You'll find out that this messenger wasn't happy that the people were paying attention and trying to please God.

Maybe you don't like it when someone you know starts making better choices. Maybe you feel better about the choices you make when you know someone else is making choices that are not as good as yours. Anyone thinking this way needs to know God wants everyone to choose to do right.

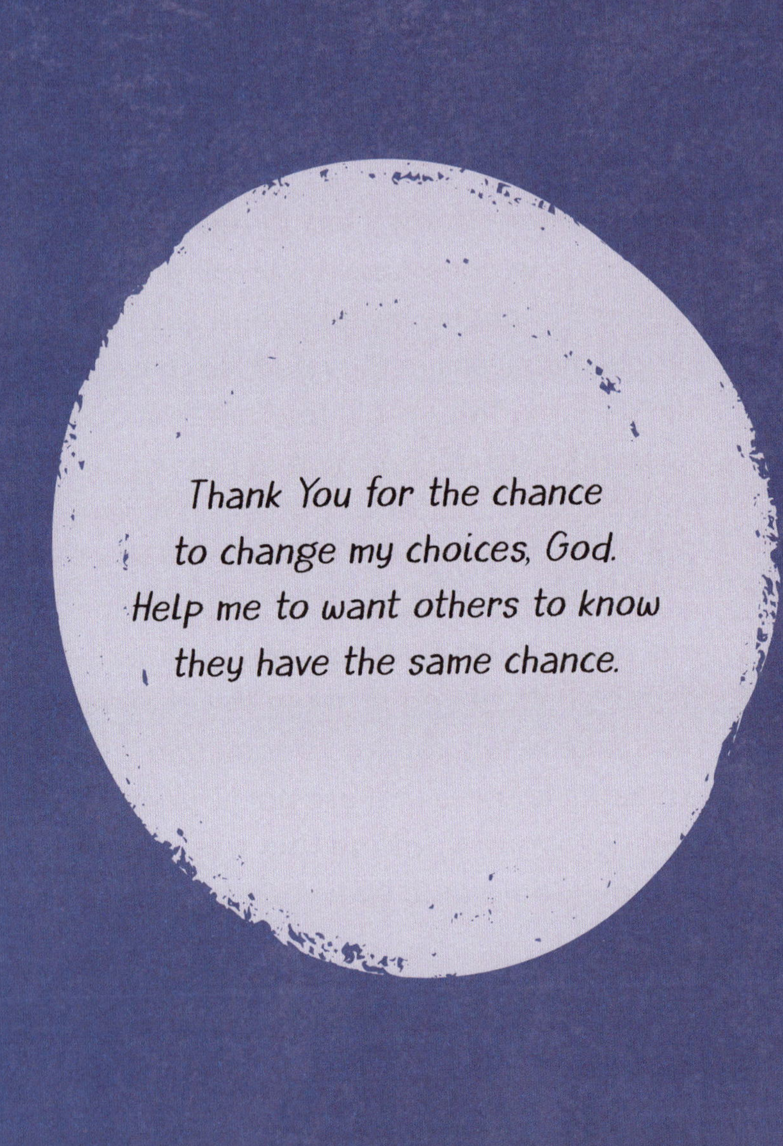
Thank You for the chance
to change my choices, God.
Help me to want others to know
they have the same chance.

FAITHFUL FIRST

If we have no faith, He will still be faithful for He cannot go against what He is.

2 Timothy 2:13 NLV

Jonah didn't start his journey willing to be useful to God. He hadn't been faithful. The king of Nineveh and the people who lived there hadn't followed God and had been making very bad choices. These people became faithful.

God could be trusted to do the right thing, even when no one else was faithful. Before Jonah said, "No," and again after the king said, "Yes," God was faithful. He is always faithful. Always.

This is important because God was not commanding something that He hadn't shown Jonah. God is always an excellent example. In fact, He's perfect. He wants you to love, so He loved first. He wants you to forgive, so He forgave first. He wants you to be faithful, so He was faithful first.

Pay attention to what God has done and remember that He can help you become faithful, too. If you fail, remember that He can help you become faithful again.

I want to be faithful, Father.
I want the things I say and do
to sound and be like something
You would say and do. Thanks
for being the perfect example.
Help me to live out what I'm
learning about faithfulness.

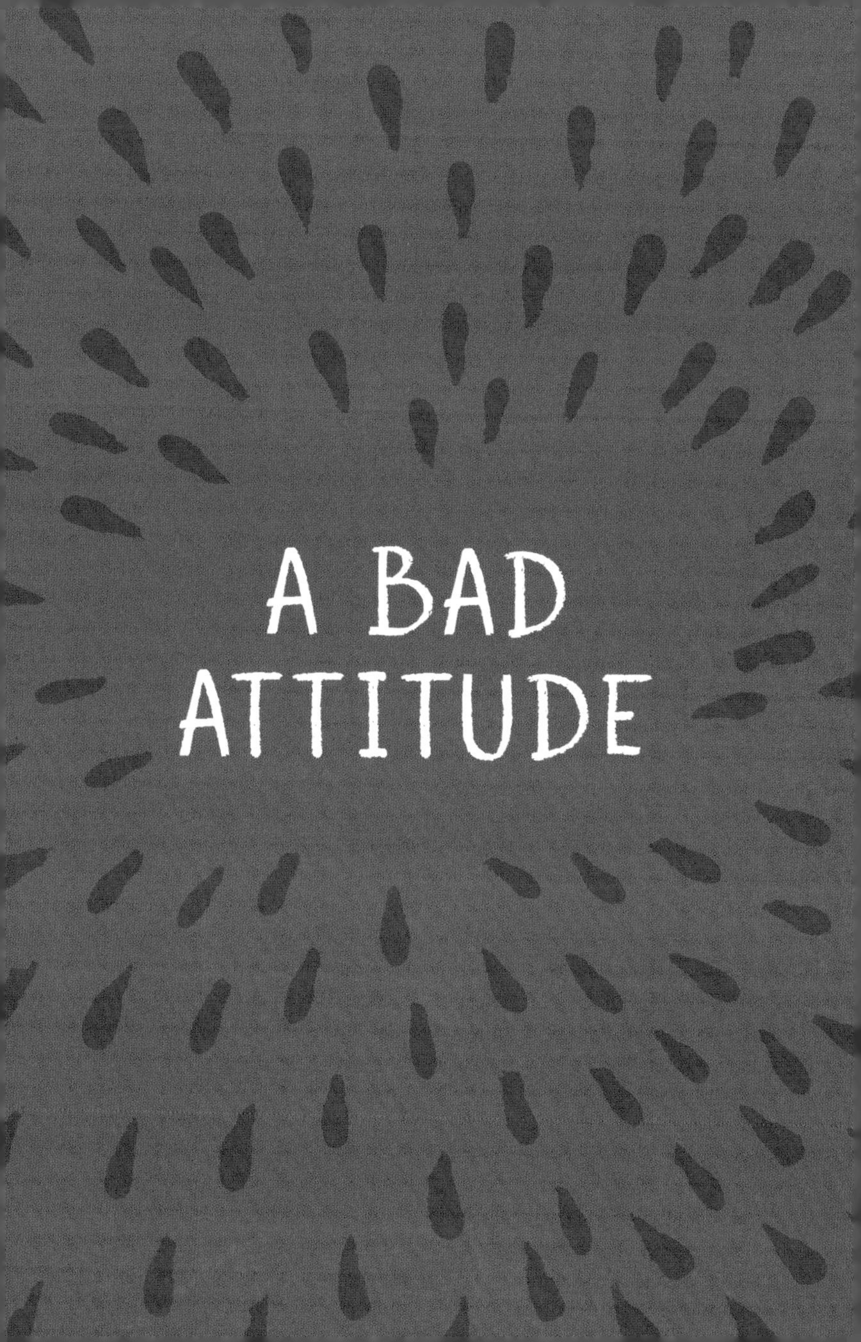
A BAD
ATTITUDE

IN CHARGE

[God's mercy] displeased Jonah. . .
and he was very angry.

Jonah 4:1 SKJV

God chose to forgive the people of Nineveh. This was wonderful news, unless you were Jonah. He gave the message that helped the people agree to change. But he didn't really want them to change. Jonah wanted these people, his country's enemies, to be punished. That's why he ran away in the first place. When that didn't work, Jonah gave the message and hoped they wouldn't listen. But they did. That made Jonah mad.

Have you ever been mad when someone did the right thing? Maybe you thought that they had done enough wrong things that they should be punished and not forgiven. Maybe you thought one right decision couldn't change the fact that they did more bad things than good. But God gave mercy to you, so why shouldn't He do the same for others?

The people of Nineveh responded to God. It was a good thing that Jonah wasn't in charge of handing out mercy.

It seems strange, but Jonah didn't seem to think that God knew what He was doing. But God knew that if Jonah were in charge, he would have made the wrong choice. Here's good news: Jonah wasn't in charge.

If I ever think that You've made a mistake Lord, remind me that I don't understand everything that You know. Help me to remember that love, forgiveness, and mercy are three of Your favorite gifts. I want to be happy when You give these gifts to other people.

The Lord said, "Have you any reason to be angry?"

JONAH 4:4 NLV

Jonah was angry. But God asked if the prophet had a reason to be mad. God knew the answer. Jonah didn't have a good reason.

This prophet who had been asked to take a message to Nineveh still hoped that punishment was coming to the people who lived there. He found a place outside the city where he watched. He hoped that the people would still be punished. So Jonah waited. Jonah wondered. Jonah whined.

God made a plant grow. It shaded Jonah while he waited. That was very kind of God. The next day a worm ate away at the plant. A hot wind caused what was left to dry up and die. This also made Jonah very angry. The people were not punished, the plant died, and it was too hot and windy. Jonah was so unhappy that he told God it would be better if he had never been born. Nothing happened the way Jonah thought it should.

Have you ever been frustrated by the way things turn out? Has it ever made you sad and mad at the same time? What would be a better choice?

I think I'd be happy if
everything I wanted came true,
God. But You know better.
I want to learn to accept Your
choices for my life and the lives
of everyone I'll ever meet.

PITY PARTY

God said to Jonah, "Do you have a good reason to be angry about the plant?" And Jonah said, "I have a good reason to be angry, angry enough to die."

JONAH 4:9 NLV

Jonah was still angry.

He had been angry that God asked him to do something he didn't want to do. Then God was kind to people he didn't like. Jonah felt angry because the people of Nineveh weren't punished.

Now He got angry because God allowed a plant to die. Jonah was having a pity party. He was full of boo-hoo juice. He thought he had every right to be angry. He even thought he would rather die than change his choices.

You may remember that God was unhappy with the sins of the people of Nineveh. But He was filled with joy when they turned to faith in Him. Jonah felt happy about the bad choices of the people of Nineveh. The prophet became unhappy when they decided to choose God's way. Jonah did not choose the same way God did.

Ask yourself if the way you choose is what God has asked you to choose. If not, then ask yourself who might be wrong.

When things don't go my way, Father, help me to see if they are going Your way. If they are, let my anger turn to joy. I can know that good things are coming because You always make good choices.

JUDGMENT AND REWARDS

[God said,] "Should not I spare Nineveh, that great city, in which are more than one hundred and twenty thousand persons who cannot discern between their right hand and their left hand?"

JONAH 4:11 SKJV

God kindly gave Jonah a plant for shade. He didn't have to do that. Jonah was happy to accept this mercy from a good God.

Jonah remained angry that God was showing kindness to Nineveh. God explained His choice to rescue Nineveh in words that Jonah should have understood. More than one hundred thousand people lived in Nineveh. That included children, parents, and grandparents. There were some men and women who loved their families and wanted good things for them.

There were people who were lost and uncertain. God wanted to change their lives so they would love Him. So God sent Jonah. But Jonah had no use for these people.

Some people think that every bad thing others do should be punished. But they don't want God to punish their own sins. They think good things should be rewarded, except when someone they don't like is rewarded. Here's an interesting truth: God often corrects bad choices with kindness—first.

Help me to be willing to wait to see the good You bring, Lord. It's easy to see the bad in others and wonder why You don't correct them quickly. Remind me that sometimes You make a bigger change with Your mercy. Then everything is made right with Your forgiveness.

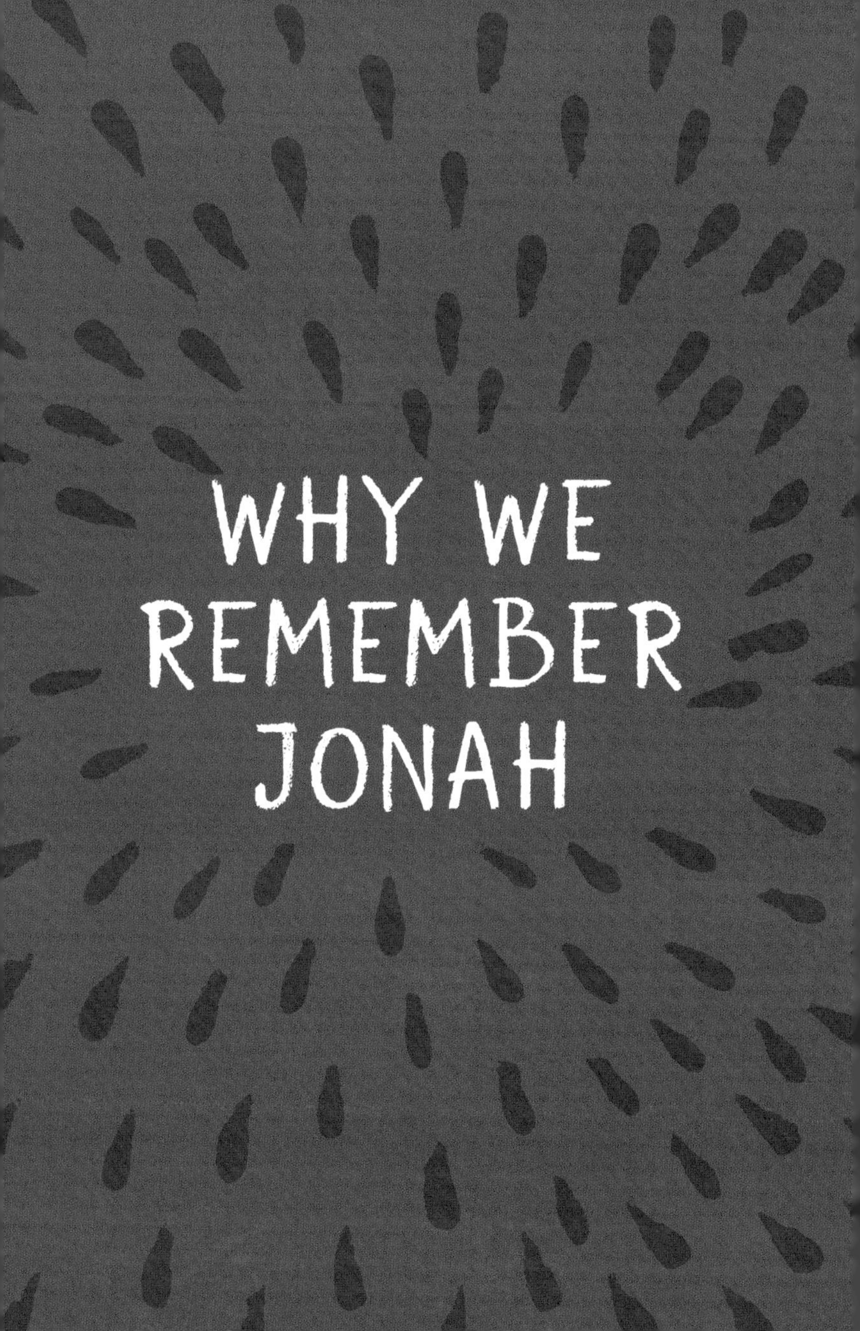
WHY WE
REMEMBER
JONAH

A LOT LIKE YOU

The Word of the Lord came to Jonah the son of Amittai.

Jonah 1:1 NLV

Jonah must have been faithful before God asked him to deliver a message to the city of Nineveh. The prophet wasn't always against God. Jonah might even have thought that if he did not take the message to Nineveh, the people would be corrected. After all, isn't that what God wanted?

One of the ways we remember Jonah is that he was disobedient—and he was. He may not have thought that was what he was doing. But we can all make that mistake. You might believe it's a good idea not to do something you know God wants you to do. But you may not believe your disobedience really matters. You might even think your bad choice is helpful. But it will never help if it's not what God wants.

Jonah was very much like every person who has ever lived. He knew what God wanted, and he didn't want to do it. Any one of us can know what God wants and run the other way.

It's easy to think the worst about Jonah, but it can be like looking into the mirror.

*Help me to honor You,
tell the truth, and forgive
others, God. It's a short list
but a great start. I want to
learn from Jonah so I know
what to do and not to do.*

WHEN TROUBLES GROW

[Jonah said to God,] "When my soul fainted within me, I remembered the Lord, and my prayer came in to You, into Your holy temple."

Jonah 2:7 SKJV

When Jonah was thrown into the sea, his troubles grew. A giant fish swallowed him whole. How could Jonah expect to escape the belly of a big fish? He had disobeyed God. Would God help Him?

In the fish's belly Jonah must have thought about his choices. He soon remembered that every good thing comes from God. So Jonah prayed to the God who could help him see sunlight and breathe fresh air again.

We remember Jonah because when things seem to be the worst they have ever been, God is the only one who can bring hope. When that happened to Jonah, he prayed.

Jonah wasn't perfect. He proved he could make more than one bad decision. But when life was the most difficult, Jonah knew where to turn for help, answers, and hope.

When you have really bad days, do what Jonah did—pray. God listens, even when the one doing the praying is good at making bad choices.

Thank You for the reminder that You want to hear from me even on '"bad choice" days, Father. Make me smart enough to get in touch and stay in touch when I do wrong. Help me to follow You.

[God said to Jonah,]
"Get up and go. . . ."
So Jonah got up and went.

JONAH 3:2–3 NLV

Praying helped clear things up for Jonah. There was a moment when God gave Jonah a second chance. And the prophet chose to turn around and make the long trip to Nineveh. If it took the same amount of time to walk through Nineveh as it did for him to be in the belly of a big fish, he would do it.

He stopped disobeying God and simply got up and went where God sent him.

You may know that God wants you to honor your parents, but sometimes you choose not to. You know God doesn't want you to lie, yet sometimes that is exactly what you do. You know God wants you to forgive, but you'd rather see someone punished. If this is a sickness, then Jonah had caught it, too.

There was a moment when Jonah recovered and obeyed. This act of obedience was used by God even when Jonah slipped back into bad attitudes. You can learn from your own bad choices, or you can learn from Jonah. However you learn the lesson, just do what God says!

When I obey, it could help someone else, Lord. Even if I don't feel as if it's something that will help me, I want to obey because You asked. You made me and give me jobs to do. The least I can do is obey.

“THREE DAYS” DIFFERENCE

[Jesus said,] “For as Jonah was three days and three nights in the whale’s belly, so shall the Son of Man be three days and three nights in the heart of the earth.”

MATTHEW 12:40 SKJV

Jesus remembered Jonah. He once taught those around Him that the picture of Jonah inside the belly of the fish for three days was very much as it would be for Him. Jesus would be in a tomb for three days, but when He left, things would change for people who listened to what He said and did what He asked.

Jonah saw how over a hundred thousand people could change because of what he had learned over three days. It meant people could be better parents, friends, and neighbors. They would have a chance to get to know God. They could choose love over hate.

Jesus walked out of His own tomb. Those three days prepared Him for a rescue plan that is still offered today. Nothing would be the same.

Did you think Jonah's story was cool? Then you need to know it's a story that can help you understand Jesus even better.

Heavenly Father, help me to remember that I don't have to make bad decisions like Jonah's to know that obedience is the very best idea.